EARTH FILES

EARTH FILES – FORESTS
was produced by

David West Children's Books
7 Princeton Court
55 Felsham Road
London SW15 1AZ

Editor: James Pickering
Picture Research: Carrie Haines

First published in Great Britain in 2002 by
Heinemann Library, Halley Court, Jordan Hill, Oxford OX2 8EJ, a division of Reed Educational and Professional Publishing Limited.

OXFORD MELBOURNE AUCKLAND
JOHANNESBURG BLANTYRE GABORONE
IBADAN PORTSMOUTH (NH) USA CHICAGO

06 05 04 03 02
10 9 8 7 6 5 4 3 2 1

ISBN 0 431 15625 5 (HB)
ISBN 0 431 15632 8 (PB)

British Library Cataloguing in Publication Data

Ganeri, Anita
Forests. - (Earth Files)
1. Forests and forestry - Juvenile literature
2. Forest ecology - Juvenile literature
I. Title
577.3

Printed and bound in Italy

PHOTO CREDITS :
Abbreviations: t-top, m-middle, b-bottom, r-right, l-left, c-centre.

Front cover, 3 & 29tl, 4t, 5tr & 12tr, 5b & 22bl, 6b, 6-7b, 7b, 15tl & ml, 16bl, 17tl, 20tr, bl & br, 21tl, bl & br, 27tr, 28tr, 29ml - Corbis Images. 4b & 19bl, 17br - Roger Vlitos. 8bl (Jean-Paul Ferrero), 8tr (Adrian Warren), 9br, 12-13 (D.W. Napier), 10br, 29br (François Gohier), 12bl (Bob Gibbons), 13tr (Yves Bilat), 13bl (Pascal Goetgheluck), 14tr (M. Watson), 14br (Keith & Liz Laidler), 15br (Nick Gordon), 16-17t (Chris Knights), 18-19b (Masahiro Iijima), 20tl (Yack A. Bailey), 21tr (Jim Zipp), 24bl (Piers Cavendish), 24-25t (David Dixon), 25bl (Kenneth W. Fink), 25br (Joanna van Gruisen), 29bl (Mary Clay), 9tr, 18tr, 19tr - Ardea London Ltd. 10tr (E.J. Bent), 11tr, 27br, 28br (Wayne Lawler), 11br (Dave Wootton), 24br (Simon Grove), 28bl (Rob Nichol) - Ecoscene. 22tr (David Beatty), 23tr (IMS/Roland Andersson), 23br (R. Hanbury-Tenison), 23tl, 26bl, 26-27t - Robert Harding Picture Library.

An explanation of difficult words can be found in the glossary on page 31.

EARTH FILES

Anita Ganeri

CONTENTS

6 WORLD FORESTS

8 TROPICAL RAINFORESTS

10 RAINFOREST PLANTS

12 RAINFOREST RELATIONSHIPS

14 JUNGLES OF SOUTH AMERICA

16 TEMPERATE WOODLANDS

18 FORESTS OF THE NORTH

20 LIFE IN THE FOREST

22 FOREST PEOPLE

24 ESSENTIAL FORESTS

26 FOREST RESOURCES

28 FORESTS IN DANGER

30 AMAZING FOREST FACTS

31 GLOSSARY

32 INDEX

Temperate rainforests grow along the west coast of the USA. They contain giant sequoias and redwoods, some of the tallest trees on Earth.

INTRODUCTION

From vast conifer woodlands in the far north, to hot, steamy jungles near the Equator, forests are vitally important. They provide us with resources, such as food, timber and medicines. Tropical rainforests alone are home to at least half of all the world's species of plants and animals, with many more waiting to be discovered. Ten thousand years ago, forests covered half of the Earth. Today, they are disappearing fast. In recent years, deforestation has become one of the most serious problems facing our planet.

Forests provide a rich food supply for animals such as fruit bats.

Great forests of conifer trees stretch across the far north of North America, Asia and Europe.

Traditionally, rainforest people live in harmony with nature. Today, their life and culture is under threat.

WORLD FORESTS

Forests grow all over the world, covering about a third of the Earth's land surface. They range from dry, scrubby forests scattered across the African savannah to tangled swamps of mangroves along tropical coasts.

Temperate woodland
Temperate woodland grows mainly in the northern hemisphere.

FOREST TREES AND TYPES

There are three main types of forest – tropical, boreal and temperate. Tropical forests grow along the Equator, in South America, Africa and Asia. Smaller patches are found in Australia and the Caribbean. Boreal forests grow in the cold, dry north where the winters are long and harsh. Temperate forests are found in places which have a moderate climate, with warm summers and cool winters.

Tropical rainforest
The world's largest rainforest grows along the banks of the Amazon River.

A mixture of broad-leaved and coniferous trees grow in temperate forests. Many broad-leaved trees are deciduous.

Boreal (northern) forests are dominated by conifers – trees that are adapted to withstand the cold, harsh climate.

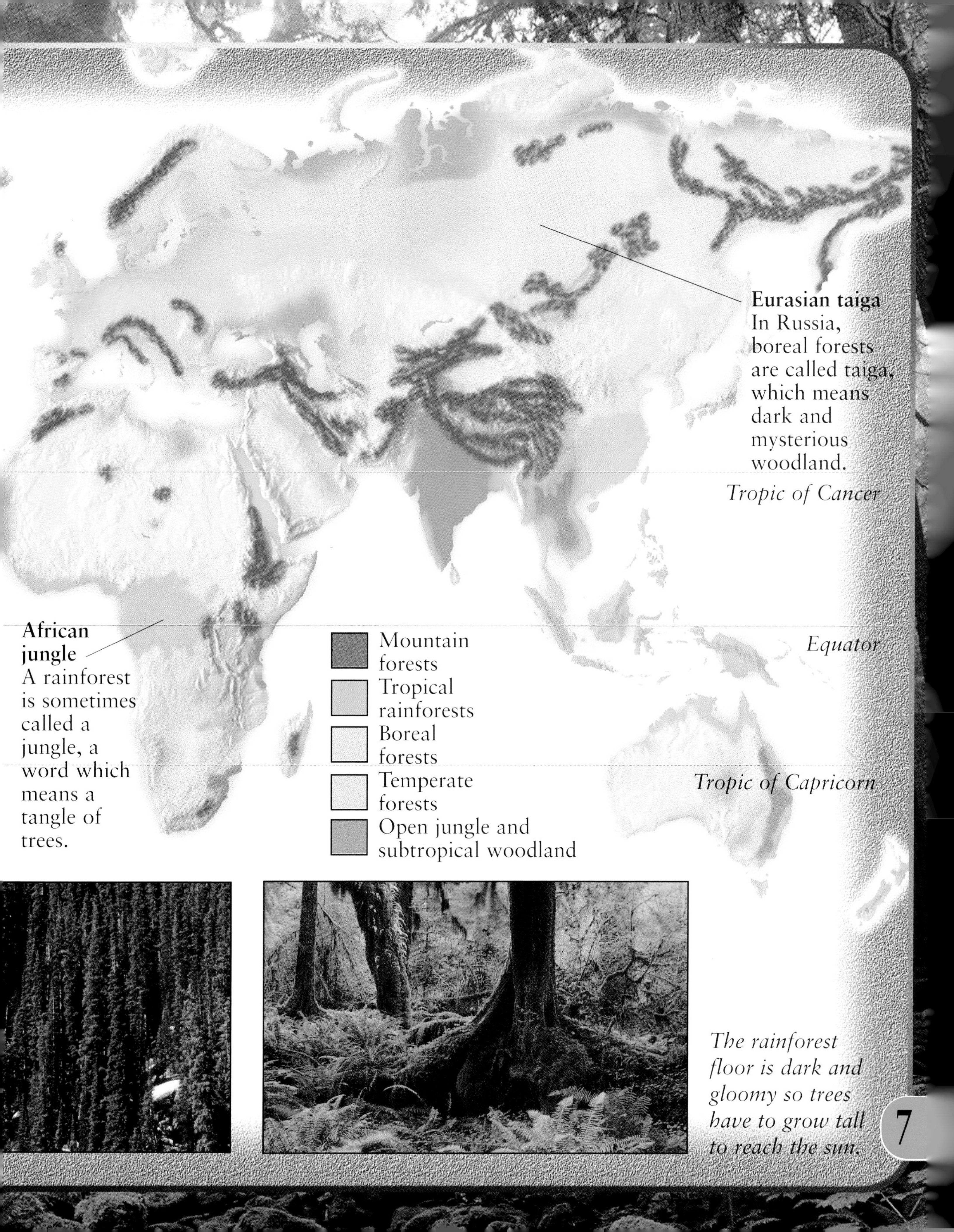

The rainforest floor is dark and gloomy so trees have to grow tall to reach the sun.

TROPICAL RAINFORESTS

Tropical rainforests cover about six per cent of the Earth's land surface. All rainforests are hot, wet and humid but there are different types, depending on where they grow.

Cloud forest in Rwanda.

RAINFOREST CLIMATE

Rainforests grow along the Equator where the climate is hot and humid all year round, with average temperatures of 20–28°C. There is rain almost every day, with frequent thunderstorms in the afternoons. The combination of heat and moisture is ideal for plants to grow.

Lowland tropical rainforest in Borneo.

TYPES OF RAINFOREST

Montane forest

Montane forests grow high up on the sides of tropical mountains. The forests are also known as 'cloud forests', because they are often shrouded in mist.

Lowland forest

Most rainforests grow on low-lying land. The treetops form a thick canopy above the forest floor.

Rainforest soils

Despite the large number of trees that grow there, rainforest soils are surprisingly poor. The goodness in the soil, called nutrients, are quickly washed away by the rain. Plants overcome this problem by growing spreading, shallow roots. These suck up goodness from the upper layers of soil before it is lost.

Monkey puzzles

The first rainforests grew about 150 million years ago. Ancient rainforest trees included monkey-puzzle trees, a type of conifer which still grows today. Small forests of monkey-puzzles grow in south-eastern Chile.

Monkey-puzzle forest, Chile.

Flooded forest

Large parts of lowland forests are flooded when a river bursts its banks. Some shrubs and plants spend most of the year underwater.

River

Flood plain

Mangrove forests

Huge, muddy swamps grow where tropical rivers meet the sea. These support forests of mangrove trees.

Mangrove swamp.

RAINFOREST PLANTS

A huge variety of plants and trees grows in the rainforest. In a patch of forest the size of a soccer pitch, there may be 200 kinds of tree, compared to ten in a temperate forest.

TREE FEATURES

Rainforest trees grow in layers, depending on their height. Competition for light is fierce, so some trees grow very tall. Trees need sunlight for photosynthesis. This is the process by which green plants make food, using the energy from sunlight to combine water and carbon dioxide.

Emergent trees are battered by storms and high winds.

Banyan trees have long, spreading roots which hang down from their trunks. Banyans are a type of fig tree.

Some rainforest trees grow huge buttress roots to help support their tall trunks. The roots may reach 9 metres up the tree's trunk.

Forest floor

The forest floor gets little sunlight and is dark and gloomy. It is covered with fungi, ferns, mosses and rotting leaves.

RAINFOREST LAYERS

Emergents

A few, very tall trees grow up to 60 metres above the ground. Their crowns poke up above the canopy below.

Orchids and bromeliads grow on tree branches. Their dangling roots suck moisture from the air.

Canopy

In the canopy, a mass of treetops forms a thick, green roof several metres thick above the forest floor. Moisture is trapped in the canopy.

Understorey

The understorey is made up of small trees such as palms and saplings which sprout in the gaps left by fallen trees.

Giant flowers

The world's largest flower, the rafflesia, grows in the rainforests of Borneo and Sumatra. It measures up to a metre across and smells of rotten meat. Its terrible smell attracts insects for pollination.

Rafflesia flower.

RAINFOREST RELATIONSHIPS

At least half of all the world's species of plants and animals live in the rainforests. The plants and animals of the rainforest community are closely linked, each with their own particular job to do.

SEED DISPERSAL

Animals play a vital part in spreading plants' seeds. Plants need to spread their seeds so that they can find a good place to grow. To attract animals, plants grow tasty fruits. The animals spit the seeds out or swallow them, and pass them out in their droppings.

This 'ant plant' has a large swollen stem with a network of tunnels that have ants living inside them.

Fruit-eating bats help to spread the seeds of many rainforest plants. They like fruits with a musty smell.

ANT PLANTS

Some plants have ants growing inside their leaves, stems and thorns. The ants and plants usually help each other. The plants provide the ants with food and shelter, while the ants attack any animals who try to eat the plants.

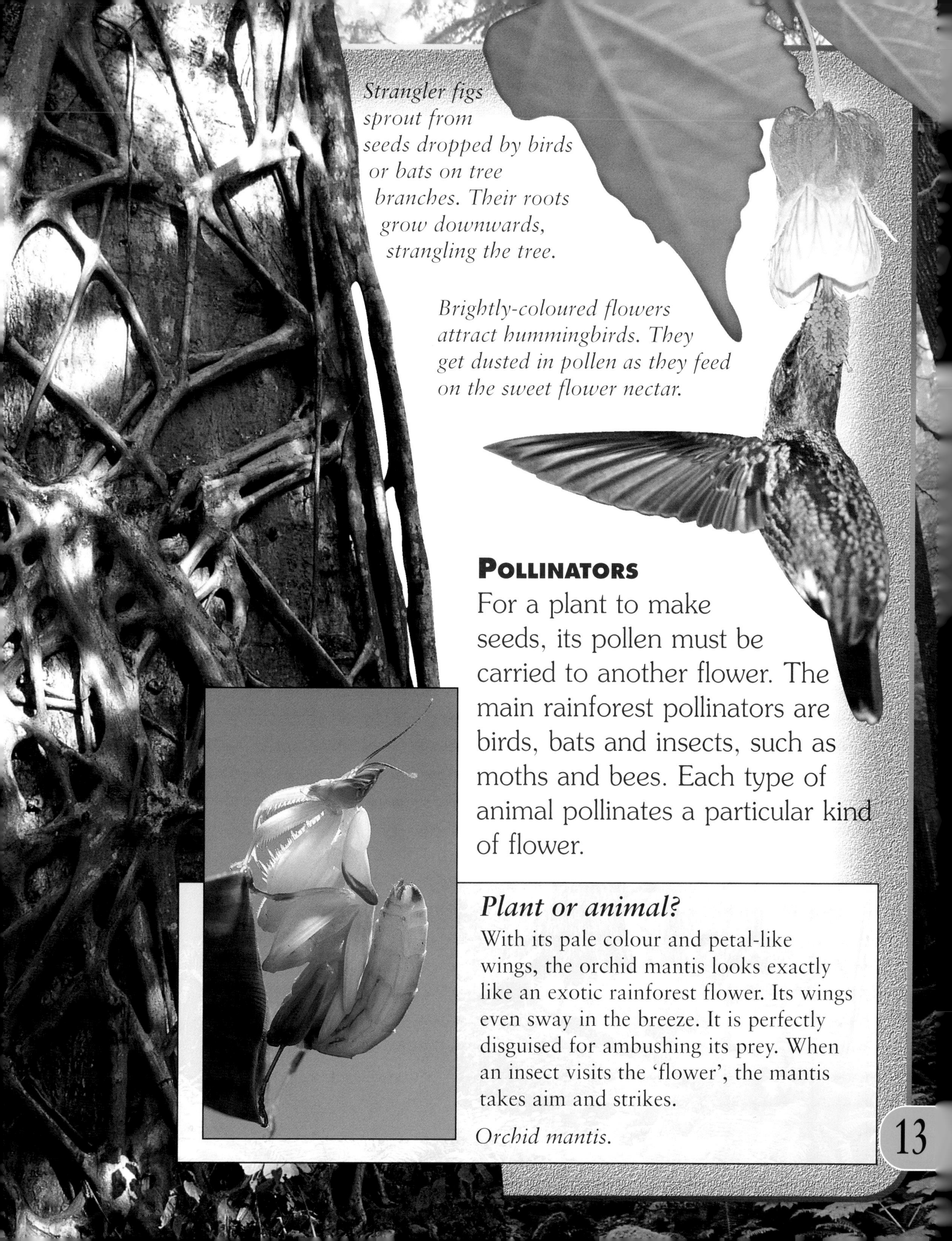

Strangler figs sprout from seeds dropped by birds or bats on tree branches. Their roots grow downwards, strangling the tree.

Brightly-coloured flowers attract hummingbirds. They get dusted in pollen as they feed on the sweet flower nectar.

Pollinators

For a plant to make seeds, its pollen must be carried to another flower. The main rainforest pollinators are birds, bats and insects, such as moths and bees. Each type of animal pollinates a particular kind of flower.

Plant or animal?

With its pale colour and petal-like wings, the orchid mantis looks exactly like an exotic rainforest flower. Its wings even sway in the breeze. It is perfectly disguised for ambushing its prey. When an insect visits the 'flower', the mantis takes aim and strikes.

Orchid mantis.

JUNGLES OF SOUTH AMERICA

The vast rainforests of South America stretch from Venezuela in the north to Argentina in the south. The world's biggest rainforest grows along the Amazon River in Brazil, covering six million square kilometres.

Canopy creatures
Sloths are perfectly adapted for life in the canopy. They hang upside-down in the trees, gripping the branches with their hook-like claws. They rarely come to the ground.

CANOPY LIFE

The rainforest canopy receives more light and rain than any other part of the forest. It is home to the majority of rainforest animals, including monkeys, snakes, sloths and frogs.

THE AMAZON

The mighty Amazon River flows for about 6,400 kilometres through South America. It begins in the Andes Mountains of Peru and flows into the Atlantic Ocean in Brazil. The Amazon has more than 1,000 known tributaries and contains more water than any other river on Earth.

ATLANTIC OCEAN
River Amazon
Amazon rainforest
Andes
SOUTH AMERICA

River life
The giant anaconda is an excellent swimmer, preying on animals that come to the river to drink.

Monkey-eating eagles
Huge eagles live and nest among the crowns of the tallest rainforest trees. They swoop down on monkeys in the canopy beneath.

Jungle hunters

The most feared jungle hunter is the jaguar. It patrols the forest floor, searching for prey, such as deer, wild pigs and tapirs. It sometimes drops down on prey from the branch of a tree. Jaguars are also good swimmers, chasing after alligators and fish.

Deadly frogs
Tiny frogs live in the canopy. Their brightly-coloured skin contains a deadly poison. Local people use it to tip their hunting arrows.

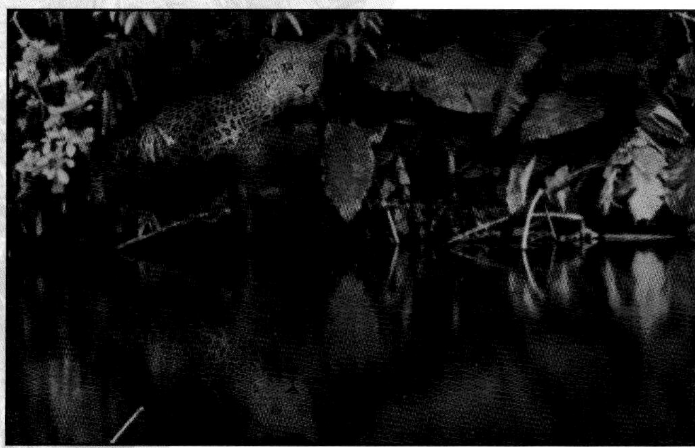

Forest floor
Shade-loving plants, such as mosses, ferns and fungi, thrive on the forest floor. Hunters, such as jaguars, also lurk there.

Flooded forest

After heavy rainfall, the Amazon River and its tributaries may burst their banks and flood the forest. Low-lying plants may spend months underwater. When the water goes down, they quickly grow flowers and fruits before they are submerged once more.

Flooded forest.

TEMPERATE WOODLANDS

Temperate forests grow in places with cool winters, warm summers and fairly steady amounts of rainfall throughout the year. They are mostly found in the northern hemisphere, in Europe, North America, China and Japan.

TEMPERATE TREES

The main types of tree in a temperate forest are broad-leaved trees, such as beech, oak, elm, maples and hickories. But some forests contain a mixture of conifers and broad-leaved trees.

In autumn, the leaves turn from green to brilliant reds and golds as they stop photosynthesising for winter.

NUTRIENT CYCLES

In a forest, nothing goes to waste. Everything is recycled, and used again and again. When plants and animals die (1 and 2), bacteria, fungi, earthworms and insects in the soil feed on their bodies and break them down (3). This process transfers the nutrients, or goodness, the plants and animals contain into the soil. Forest plants take the nutrients up through their roots and use them to grow (4). Animals feed on the plants, and the whole cycle begins again.

The forest floor is covered in rich leaf-litter which provides food for earthworms and insects. Plants, such as bluebells and ferns, thrive in the cool shade.

Changing seasons

The changing of the seasons is very marked in a temperate forest. Many broad-leaved trees are deciduous which means they lose their leaves in winter when the ground is frozen and there is too little light for photosynthesis. The main growing season is spring and summer when the trees burst into bud, and grow flowers and fruit.

Giant trees

The biggest living things on Earth are massive giant sequoia trees. They grow in the temperate rainforests, along the west coast of North America. Giant sequoias can weigh over 1,000 tonnes and stand over 90 metres tall. Their bark alone can be almost a metre thick.

Giant seqouia.

FORESTS OF THE NORTH

Boreal, or northern, forests stretch in a huge band across the far north of Europe, Asia and North America. They grow up to the treeline, beyond which it is too cold and windy for trees to grow.

Cold climate

Boreal forests are the coldest, driest forests. Winters are long and extremely cold, with temperatures falling as low as -70°C and heavy snowfall. Summers are warm but last for just a few months. This only allows a short growing season for plants and trees.

Tough trees

Trees have to be tough to cope with life in the cold. Most of the trees in the northern forests are evergreen conifers, such as pine, spruce, cedar and redwoods. Some forests also have a few deciduous broad-leaved trees, such as birches and willows, which are hardy enough to survive.

A conifer tree's sloping shape allows heavy snow to slide off its branches, without damaging the tree.

Adapting to conditions

Conifers are ideally suited to the cold conditions. Instead of broad leaves, conifers have fine, waxy needles that stop too much water being lost.

Conifer trees tend to grow close together for protection against the wind. They are also grown on plantations, for timber and paper pulp.

Forest fires

Forest fires sometimes happen naturally, when trees are struck by lightning. These fires spread quickly, but are useful for keeping the forest under control and encouraging new growth. Many conifers burn easily because of the resin in their wood and leaves. But other trees have developed a thick layer of bark which protects them from the flames.

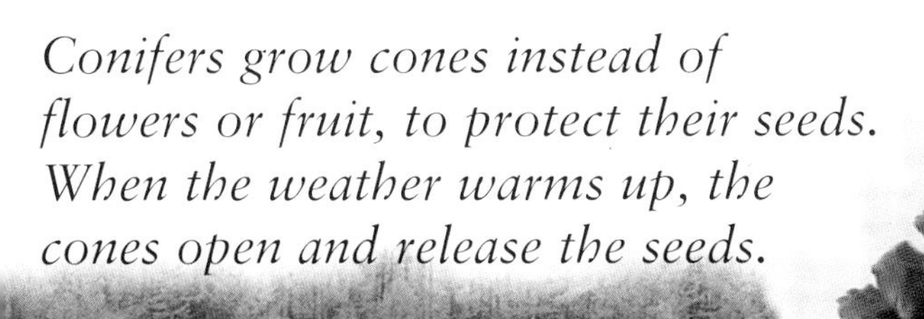

Conifers grow cones instead of flowers or fruit, to protect their seeds. When the weather warms up, the cones open and release the seeds.

LIFE IN THE FOREST

Temperate and boreal forests are not as rich in wildlife as rainforests. But the trees provide food and shelter for large numbers of animals, from insects and birds, to bats and bears.

A purple hairstreak butterfly feeding on an oak leaf.

LIFE IN AN OAK TREE

In a temperate woodland, a single oak tree can support a large community of animals. Insects are adapted for living on the tree's leaves, twigs, bark and roots. Many animals come to feed on the insects.

The American badger is smaller than its European cousin. It feeds on smaller mammals, such as squirrels.

Packs of wolves roam the northern forests, on the look-out for prey such as moose or caribou.

Grizzly bears eat roots, berries and insect grubs. They also fish for salmon in fast-flowing streams.

Koalas

Koalas live in the temperate forests of south-east Australia. They live among the eucalyptus trees, eating so many of the trees' leaves that their fur smells strongly of eucalyptus.

Koalas only feed on eucalyptus leaves.

Surviving the cold

Surviving winter in the boreal forest is very tough. The weather is cold and icy, and food is scarce. Some animals, such as squirrels, collect and hide seeds and nuts to live on. Others, such as bears, save energy by hibernating. Their heart and breathing rates slow right down and they fall into a deep sleep. They live off stores of body fat built up during autumn when there was plenty of food.

Crossbills have specially adapted beaks which cross over for prising open pine cones to reach the seeds inside.

Red deer browse, or graze, on lichens and moss on the forest floor.

The Barn owl is nocturnal. It spends the day roosting in the trees and comes out at night to hunt.

FOREST PEOPLE

People have lived in the world's forests for thousands of years. They rely on the forest for food, fuel, medicines and materials for homes and clothes.

LIVING WITH NATURE

Local people take what they need from the forest and show the forest great respect. Today, their way of life is under threat as the forests are cleared for land and timber. Settlers from outside also bring in diseases, such as measles and flu.

The Mbuti people of Zaire are expert hunters, tracking okapi and antelope through the rainforest.

The traditional way of life of the rainforest people of Papua New Guinea is threatened by the loss of their forest habitat.

The open space in the middle of the yano is used for meetings, ceremonial dancing and feasts.

Rainforest people

About 1.5 million people live in the tropical rainforests. The Yanomami people live in the Amazon rainforest. They build huge, circular houses, called yanos, in clearings in the forest. A yano is shared by about 20 families, each with its own living space.

Reindeer herders

The Saami people live in the coniferous forests of northern Norway, Sweden and Finland. They live by herding forest reindeer. The Saami rely on the reindeer for meat, milk and skins, and use them to carry heavy loads and pull sledges.

Saami reindeer herders.

FARMING THE FOREST

The Yanomami hunt game, catch fish, collect wild plants and grow their own crops. They clear a small patch of forest and plant maize, sweet potatoes, bananas and manioc. The 'gardens' are abandoned after two or three years when the goodness in the soil is used up. The plots are left so that the rainforest can grow back again. It may be 50 years before a plot can be used again. In this way, the Yanomami use the forest without doing it any lasting harm.

A Yanomami tending his garden.

Not only are forests home to millions of plants and animals, they also have a far-reaching effect on the world's weather and climate.

FORESTS AND CLIMATE

Huge stores of carbon are locked up in rainforest trees. When the forests are cut down, and rot or burn, the carbon is released into the atmosphere as carbon dioxide. Scientists are worried that this is adding to the greenhouse effect which may be making the Earth warmer.

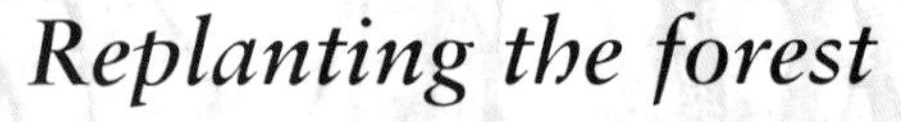

Replanting the forest

In some places, forests are being replanted. As the new trees grow, they take in carbon dioxide from the atmosphere for making food and wood. This takes back some of the carbon dioxide given out into the atmosphere when the original forest was cut down.

Replanting a forest in Thailand.

Scientists have discovered as many as 1,500 species of rainforest insects in a single tree. They shake the insects out of the tree to study them.

Until recently, exploring the canopy was very difficult. Today, scientists use lightweight metal walkways, hung many metres above the ground, to walk among the canopy trees and study the plants and animals.

Wildlife riches

For scientists, the rainforests are treasure troves of wildlife. All the time, they are discovering new species which have never been seen before. Finding out more about rainforest wildlife is very important. For example, research into rainforest plants is helping to produce disease-resistant strains of crops which can feed millions around the world.

MEDICINE CHEST

Many forest plants have medicinal qualities. About a quarter of the medicines we use come from rainforest plants. Forest people have been using these plants for years and their knowledge is helping scientists. Doctors are already using one plant, the rosy periwinkle from Madagascar, to treat some types of cancer.

Rosy periwinkle, Madagascar.

A chemical in the bark of the Pacific yew can also be used to help fight cancer.

FOREST RESOURCES

Forests, especially rainforests, are very rich in natural resources. These include timber, rubber, food, and valuable metals. We use many forest resources in our daily lives.

TIMBER

For centuries, forests have been chopped down for their wood. Today, the timber trade is worth millions of pounds a year. The most valuable trees are tropical hardwoods, such as teak and mahogany. But conifer forests are also felled for making plywood and paper.

FOOD FROM THE RAINFORESTS

Many of the foods we buy from the supermarket come from the rainforests. They include fruit, such as bananas and pineapples, nuts, such as Brazil nuts, and spices, such as pepper, ginger and cloves. The beans used to make coffee and chocolate are the seeds of rainforest trees.

Picking coffee beans.

People get rubber from trees like these by making cuts in the bark. The sticky latex oozes out and drips into a collecting bowl.

Almost all of the conifer forests of western North America have been felled for timber. These redwood logs are being floated down river to be processed at a saw mill.

Rubber tapping

Rubber is made from the white, sticky sap, called latex, from rainforest rubber trees. Most of the world's rubber comes from huge plantations in South East Asia.

Precious metals

Some rainforests are rich in valuable metals, such as gold, aluminium, iron, copper and manganese. But large-scale mining destroys huge areas of rainforest and pollutes the land. Roads built to transport miners and equipment also leave scars on the landscape.

A mine in Papua New Guinea.

FORESTS IN DANGER

All over the world, forests are being cut down. It is not only the rainforests that are in danger. The boreal forests and temperate woodlands are also vanishing.

Forest clearance

Forests are cut down for many reasons – for their timber and to clear land for growing crops and cattle ranching. Vast areas of Central American rainforest have been cleared for cattle ranching. Most of the beef produced is made into hamburgers for the USA.

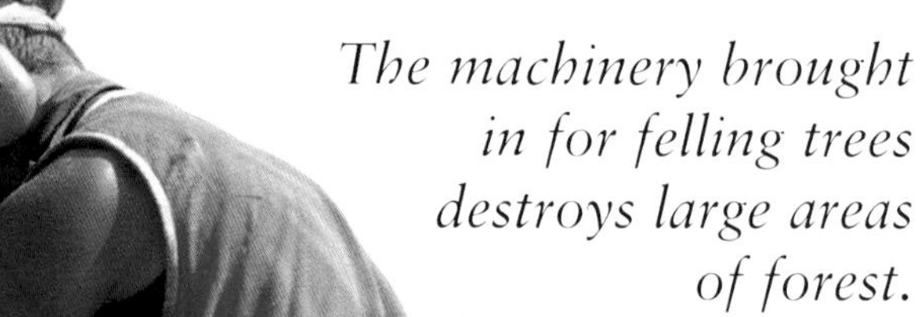

The machinery brought in for felling trees destroys large areas of forest.

Animals in danger

As their forest homes are destroyed, animals are becoming extinct at an alarming rate. It is estimated that, in the rainforests alone, at least 100 species of plants and animals are disappearing every week.

Orang-utan.

Forests in the future

Saving the forests and their precious resources has become one of the most urgent environmental concerns facing us today. All over the world, conservation groups and governments are working to halt the destruction. In some countries, forests have been made into national parks where logging, mining and hunting are banned. Replanting programmes have been started in some poorer countries, where wood from the forest is a vital source of fuel.

Tiger.

Gorilla.

Land cleared for cattle ranching is only productive for a few years. Then the ranch has to be moved on and another area of forest has to be cleared.

When a hillside is cleared of trees, there is nothing to bind the soil together. Heavy rains cause floods and landslides.

THE LARGEST FOREST	The largest forest in the world is the vast boreal forest which stretches right across the far north of North America, Russia and Europe. In places, it is 2,000 kilometres wide and measures 10,000 kilometres from one end to the other.
BIGGEST RAINFOREST	The biggest rainforest is the Amazon rainforest in Brazil. It covers six million square kilometres. But the forest is being destroyed at an alarming rate. Experts estimate that a piece of forest the size of Switzerland is being cut down every year. At this rate, in 30–50 years the forest could be gone.
WETTEST FORESTS	In most rainforests, rain falls almost every day in heavy afternoon downpours, giving about 1,800 millimetres of rain a year. The heaviest rainfall on record happens in the forests of Liberia, in Africa. Here the rain can pour down at an incredible 400 millimetres an hour.
LARGEST MANGROVE FOREST	The Sundarbans stretch for about 260 kilometres along the coast of the Bay of Bengal in India and Bangladesh. They are the largest mangrove forest in the world. The Sundarbans are one of the last remaining habitats of the rare Bengal tiger.
LARGEST TREE	Giant sequoias are conifer trees, and the most massive living things in the world. The largest is a tree called the General Sherman in Sequoia National Park, California, USA. It stands over 95 metres tall and measures more than 25 metres around its trunk. It weighs an enormous 6,000 tonnes.
RAREST FOREST ANIMALS	Among the rarest forest mammals are giant pandas. There may be only about 800 pandas left in the wild. Giant pandas live in patches of mountain forest in China, and feed on the bamboo that grows there.
WORST FOREST FIRES	In summer 1997, farmers in Indonesia lit fires to clear farmland. But the fires quickly spread out of control, destroying vast areas of rainforest. The fires raged for months, covering the region with a thick cloud of smoke. Thousands of fire-fighters struggled to put out the flames.

GLOSSARY

boreal
Another word for northern.

broad-leaved
Trees that have flat, wide leaves that fall off in winter.

deciduous
Trees which lose their leaves in the winter.

deforestation
The cutting down of a forest.

evergreen
Trees which keep their leaves all year round.

greenhouse effect
The way gases in the Earth's atmosphere, such as carbon dioxide, trap the Sun's heat, causing the Earth's surface to warm up.

manioc
A type of plant with potato-like tubers which rainforest people make into flour, bread and beer.

photosynthesis
The process by which plants make their own food, by using the energy in sunlight to combine carbon dioxide and water.

plantations
Large forests of trees which have been planted like fields of crops.

pollination
How the pollen from a male flower is taken to a female flower so that a seed can grow.

prey
Animals that are hunted for food.

savannah
Another word for grassland.

taiga
A Russian word which means dark, mysterious woodland. It is used to describe boreal forests.

tributaries
Smaller rivers and streams which flow into a main river.

Amazon River 14, 15
anaconda 14
ant plant 12
arrow-poison frog 15

banyan tree 10
barn owl 21
boreal forests, 6, 7, 18, 19
  animals and plants of 20, 21
  largest 30
  people of 23
broad-leaved trees 6, 17

cattle ranching 28, 29
conifers 4, 5, 6, 7, 19
conservation efforts 29
crossbill 21

deciduous trees 16, 17
deforestation 5, 28, 29

eucalyptus trees 21
extinction 28, 29

food from the forest 26, 27
forest fires 18, 30
fruit bat 5, 12

giant panda 30
giant sequoia 17, 30
grizzly bear 20

hibernation 21
hummingbird 13

jaguar 15

koala 21

medicinal plants 25
  Pacific yew 25
  rosy periwinkle 25
mining 27
monkey-puzzle tree 9

nutrient cycle 16, 17

oak trees 20
orchid mantis 13

pollination 11, 13

rafflesia 11
rainforests 4, 5, 6, 7, 8, 9
  Amazon 14, 15, 30
  animals of 12, 13, 14, 15, 24, 25
  cloud forest 8
  flooded forest 15
  lowland forest 8
  mangrove forest 6, 9, 30
  montane forest 8
  people of 5, 22, 23
  plants of 10, 11, 12, 13, 25
  soils of 9
red deer 21
rubber 26, 27

Saami people 23
sloth 14
strangler fig 12, 13

taiga 7
temperate forests 5, 6, 7,16, 17
  animals and plants 20, 21
timber 26, 27, 28

wolf 20